D1710238

Thank you!

BELMONT COUNTY DISTRICT LIBRARY
Purchased with funds from the
November 2013 Library Levy

ANIMAL SAFARI

Spider Monkeys

by Megan Borgert-Spaniol

BELLWETHER MEDIA • MINNEAPOLIS, MN

Note to Librarians, Teachers, and Parents:

Blastoff! Readers are carefully developed by literacy experts and combine standards-based content with developmentally appropriate text.

Level 1 provides the most support through repetition of high-frequency words, light text, predictable sentence patterns, and strong visual support.

Level 2 offers early readers a bit more challenge through varied simple sentences, increased text load, and less repetition of high-frequency words.

Level 3 advances early-fluent readers toward fluency through increased text and concept load, less reliance on visuals, longer sentences, and more literary language.

Level 4 builds reading stamina by providing more text per page, increased use of punctuation, greater variation in sentence patterns, and increasingly challenging vocabulary.

Level 5 encourages children to move from "learning to read" to "reading to learn" by providing even more text, varied writing styles, and less familiar topics.

Whichever book is right for your reader, Blastoff! Readers are the perfect books to build confidence and encourage a love of reading that will last a lifetime!

This edition first published in 2014 by Bellwether Media, Inc.

No part of this publication may be reproduced in whole or in part without written permission of the publisher.
For information regarding permission, write to Bellwether Media, Inc., Attention: Permissions Department,
5357 Penn Avenue South, Minneapolis, MN 55419.

Library of Congress Cataloging-in-Publication Data

Borgert-Spaniol, Megan, 1989- author.
 Spider Monkeys / by Megan Borgert-Spaniol.
     pages cm. – (Blastoff! Readers. Animal Safari)
 Summary: "Developed by literacy experts for students in kindergarten through grade three, this book introduces spider
monkeys to young readers through leveled text and related photos"– Provided by publisher.
 Audience: 5 to 8.
 Audience: K to grade 3.
 Includes bibliographical references and index.
 ISBN 978-1-62617-064-3 (hardcover : alk. paper)
 1. Spider monkeys–Juvenile literature. I. Title. II. Series: Blastoff! readers. 1, Animal safari.
 QL737.P915B67 2014
 599.8'58–dc23
                                                                   2013032333

Printed in the United States of America, North Mankato, MN.

Contents

What Are Spider Monkeys?

Spider monkeys are **primates**. They live in the **canopy** of **rain forests**.

They grab
branches with
their long arms
and legs.

Strong tails help
them hang
upside down.

Sometimes spider
monkeys leap
from tree to tree.

Troops

Spider monkeys travel in **troops**. They call to one another with barks and other sounds.

Troops **forage** for fruits during the day. They also eat seeds, nuts, and leaves.

A spider monkey warns the troop of danger. Pumas, jaguars, and eagles are **predators**.

Mom and Baby

A female spider monkey cares for her baby. They stay together for about one year.

Mom carries her young as she swings on branches. What a ride!

Glossary

canopy—a covering formed by the tops of trees

forage—to search for food

predators—animals that hunt other animals for food

primates—animals that can use their hands to grasp food and other objects; primates are related to humans.

rain forests—warm, wet forests that get a lot of rain

troops—groups of spider monkeys that live and travel together

To Learn More

AT THE LIBRARY

Gosman, Gillian. *Spider Monkeys*. New York, N.Y.: PowerKids Press, 2012.

Schreiber, Anne. *Monkeys*. Washington, D.C.: National Geographic, 2013.

Worth, Bonnie. *If I Ran the Rain Forest*. New York, N.Y.: Random House, 2003.

ON THE WEB

Learning more about spider monkeys is as easy as 1, 2, 3.

1. Go to www.factsurfer.com.

2. Enter "spider monkeys" into the search box.

3. Click the "Surf" button and you will see a list of related Web sites.

With factsurfer.com, finding more information is just a click away.

Index

The images in this book are reproduced through the courtesy of: Nazzu, front cover; David Kilpatrick/ Alamy, p. 5; TUNS/ Glow Images, p. 7; P. Wegner/ Arco Images/ Alamy, p. 9; Sean Caffrey/ Getty Images, p. 11; Kerstiny, pp. 13, 19; Anton Ivanov, p. 15; leungchopan, p. 15 (bottom left); Diana Taliun, p. 15 (bottom middle); adistock, p. 15 (bottom right); pjjones, p.17; Eduard Kyslynskyy, p. 17 (bottom left); Rechitan Sorin, p. 17 (bottom middle); worldswildlifewonders, p. 17 (bottom right); Roland Seitre/ Nature Picture Library, p. 21.